I0492736

Central Intelligence Agency
Office of Privacy and Civil Liberties

**Review of Procedures and Practices of CIA to
Disseminate United States Person Information Acquired
Pursuant to Titles I and III and Section 702 of the
Foreign Intelligence Surveillance Act (FISA)**

August 2017

This page is intentionally blank.

Review of Procedures and Practices of CIA to Disseminate United States Person Information Acquired Pursuant to Titles I and III and Section 702 of the Foreign Intelligence Surveillance Act (FISA)

I.   Executive Summary

This report responds to the Director of National Intelligence's request that civil liberties and privacy officers for the Office of the Director of National Intelligence (ODNI), National Security Agency (NSA), Central Intelligence Agency (CIA), and Federal Bureau of Investigation (FBI) review the procedures and practices to disseminate United States (U.S.) person information acquired pursuant to Titles I/III and Section 702 of the Foreign Intelligence Surveillance Act of 1978, as amended (FISA).[1] This report was undertaken by the CIA's Office of Privacy and Civil Liberties (OPCL).

With very limited exceptions for certain activities, CIA does not conduct electronic surveillance or physical searches in the United States.[2] As such, CIA does not conduct acquisition pursuant to Section 702 of FISA, electronic surveillance pursuant to Title I of FISA, nor physical searches pursuant to Title III of FISA. CIA is, however, authorized to receive, review, and appropriately disseminate certain data acquired pursuant to Section 702 or Titles I/III that have been initially collected by FBI or NSA. As described below, such information is required to be handled under Foreign Intelligence Surveillance Court (FISC)-approved "minimization procedures" that govern the access to, retention of, and dissemination of FISA-acquired data.

This report details CIA OPCL's review of (1) CIA's procedures regarding the dissemination of U.S. person information acquired under the specified provisions of FISA; (2) CIA's actual dissemination practices in light of these procedures; (3) the training program with respect to such dissemination practices; and (4) the related compliance and oversight activities conducted by the CIA Office of General Counsel (OGC), CIA's FISA Program Office, the Department of Justice (DOJ), and ODNI.

---

[1] 50 U.S.C. §§ 1801-1885c (2008).

[2] *See* Executive Order 12333, Section 2.4(a) and (b). CIA has limited authority to conduct electronic surveillance in the United States for testing and training purposes or to conduct countermeasures to hostile electronic surveillance, as well as physical searches of non-U.S. persons' personal property that is already lawfully in CIA's possession. A description of the limited electronic surveillance and physical search activities that may be conducted within the United States may be found in Sections 4.4.1, 4.4.3, and 4.4.4 of CIA's Executive Order 12333 Attorney General Procedures, *available at* https://www.cia.gov/about-cia/privacy-and-civil-liberties/CIA-AG-Guidelines-Signed.pdf.

As detailed in this report, OPCL's review of CIA's procedures and practices with respect to the dissemination of U.S. persons found:

- CIA has specific procedures to minimize the dissemination of U.S. person information, or in other words, specific procedures to limit the dissemination of U.S person information to that which is assessed to be necessary to understand the foreign intelligence information.
- Dissemination of U.S. person information is only permitted after several prior steps to filter out irrelevant information concerning U.S. persons. The "retention decision" is a particularly critical component of this process.
- CIA requires all initial disseminations of information acquired pursuant to Titles I/III and Section 702 of FISA concerning U.S. persons to be reviewed and approved by both CIA OGC and the FISA Program Office prior to dissemination.
- Consistent with prior oversight reviews, OPCL discovered no intentional violations of CIA's procedures governing the handling and dissemination of U.S. person information.
- CIA's disseminations of FISA-acquired information concerning U.S. persons are limited in number and, when identifying a particular U.S. person, generally provided to a relatively narrow audience in order to address a specific national security threat.
  - More specifically, unlike general "strategic" information regarding broad foreign intelligence threats, CIA's disseminations of information concerning U.S. persons were "tactical" insofar as they were very often in response to requests from another U.S. intelligence agency for counterterrorism information regarding a specific individual, or in relation to a specific national security threat actor or potential or actual victim of a national security threat.
- Relatedly, because these disseminations were generally for narrow purposes and sent to a limited number of recipients, the replacement of a U.S. person identity with a generic term (e.g., "named U.S. person," sometimes colloquially referred to as "masking") was rare, due to the need to retain the U.S. person identity in order to understand the foreign intelligence information by this limited audience.
- Using a generic term in place of a U.S. person's name occurs in finished intelligence products provided to policymakers and broader audiences within the Intelligence Community, but subsequent requests to reveal the identity of the U.S. person (i.e. sometimes colloquially referred to as "unmasking") are rare. OPCL identified no such "unmaskings" in the four months of disseminations that it reviewed.

- CIA has an extensive and multi-pronged approach to training to ensure compliance with the minimization procedures.
- Compliance and oversight activities to ensure and monitor adherence to the minimization procedures are carried out by several elements of CIA, as well as DOJ, ODNI, Congress, and the FISC.

Although the clandestine mission of CIA requires the protection of sources and methods in order to protect national security, CIA also has an obligation to serve the American people by protecting the freedoms, civil liberties, and privacy rights guaranteed by the Constitution and federal laws when conducting its mission. Thus, to increase public transparency and awareness of CIA's activities, authorizations, and limitations regarding the dissemination of U.S. person information acquired under FISA, this report has been written at the unclassified level.

II. Scope of Review

In order to evaluate the scope, nature, and practices surrounding CIA's dissemination of U.S. person information acquired pursuant to Section 702 and Titles I/III of FISA, OPCL received briefings from CIA OGC, CIA's FISA Program Office, senior managers who supervise the dissemination of information outside of CIA (to include FISA-acquired information), and DOJ. OPCL reviewed the relevant CIA minimization procedures, Agency guidance, DOJ/ODNI oversight reports, and other documents regarding the dissemination of this information. Members of the OPCL staff also attended the live training provided by CIA OGC and the FISA Program Office required of all Agency personnel before they are permitted to receive access to unminimized FISA information. Finally, OPCL examined four months of CIA disseminations of U.S. person information acquired pursuant to Section 702 of FISA.

In conducting this review, OPCL examined CIA's practices and internal procedures for (1) compliance with the governing minimization procedures approved by the FISC, and (2) consistency with the comparable concepts for protecting U.S. person information embodied in the CIA's Executive Order 12333 Attorney General-approved Procedures. OPCL also employed the Fair Information Practice Principles (FIPPs)[3] to determine whether CIA's practices and procedures adequately protect U.S. persons' privacy and civil liberties. OPCL's findings are incorporated into this report.

---

[3] The FIPPS are a broadly recognized set of principles for assessing privacy impacts. For example, they have been incorporated into Executive Order 13636, Improving Critical Infrastructure Cybersecurity and the National Strategy for Trusted Identities in Cyberspace. These principles are rooted in the U.S. Department of Health, Education and Welfare's seminal 1973 report, "Records, Computers and the Rights of Citizens." The FIPPs have been implemented in the Privacy Act of 1974, with certain exemptions, including ones that apply to certain national security and law enforcement activities.

III. Background: Intelligence Collection, Retention, and Dissemination at CIA

Information shared outside of CIA is considered a dissemination, and is required to occur in accordance with approved authorities, policies, and procedures. Dissemination of information is often one of the final steps in the Intelligence Cycle, which is a six-step process through which information is converted into intelligence and made available to users. The six steps of the Intelligence Cycle include: planning and direction, collection, processing and exploitation, analysis and production, and dissemination and evaluation. Relatedly, the protections for U.S. person information begin well before CIA determines that it will share foreign intelligence information with policymakers or other partners. The protection of U.S. person information begins with the authorization to target an individual to obtain electronic communications, and extends to the controls governing the techniques used to acquire information regarding these targets, the access controls on the acquired information, and the restrictions with regard to what data may be retained and used. Only after all of these restrictions are met is it potentially permissible to disseminate acquired information concerning a U.S. person. Whether the U.S. person information in question can, in fact, be disseminated is itself a function of not only the rules governing dissemination, but also the nature of the information, the individuals or entities to which the information is to be disseminated, and the purpose for which the information is to be disseminated. As such, a general background regarding targeting, acquisition, and retention pursuant to Titles I/III and Section 702 of FISA, as well as a broad understanding of how and for what purposes CIA disseminates information, is required to fully understand CIA's dissemination practices in context.

CIA does not target individuals pursuant to Section 702 of FISA, nor does CIA conduct electronic surveillance or physical searches pursuant to Titles I/III of FISA. With limited exceptions, Executive Order 12333 prohibits CIA from conducting either electronic surveillance or physical searches within the United States.[4] CIA is, however, authorized to receive, review, and appropriately disseminate a subset of data acquired pursuant to Section 702 or Titles I/III that have been initially collected by FBI or NSA.

More specifically, CIA receives only a subset of electronic surveillance (Title I) or physical search (Title III) information initially collected by FBI.[5] In order to authorize electronic surveillance or physical search under FISA, an application approved by the Attorney General must be made by FBI to the FISC. FBI's application must include the identity of the target of the electronic surveillance or physical search if known, evidence justifying a probable cause finding that the target is a foreign power or an agent of a foreign power that uses (or is about to use) the

---

[4] *See* footnote 2.
[5] 50 U.S.C. §§ 1804, 1805, 1823, 1824.

5

communication facility (e.g., an email address) or place subject to electronic surveillance or physical search. The surveillance application is then reviewed by the FISC. If the FISC determines that probable cause has been demonstrated, the judge issues an order authorizing the electronic surveillance or physical search of the communication facilities or places specified in the application. Once authorized, FBI may only conduct the specific electronic surveillance and physical search activities authorized by the FISC, and FBI's collection activities are governed by procedures designed to minimize the acquisition of irrelevant information concerning U.S. persons.[6] If requested by FBI in certain cases, unevaluated information acquired by FBI can be shared with CIA.[7]

Under Section 702 of FISA, NSA is authorized to target only non-U.S. persons reasonably believed to be located outside the United States who are assessed to possess, communicate, or receive certain categories of foreign intelligence information authorized by the Director of National Intelligence (DNI) and the Attorney General.[8] Such targeting decisions are made by NSA personnel but are governed by "targeting procedures" that are approved by the Attorney General, in consultation with the DNI, and reviewed by the FISC.[9] CIA may nominate targets to NSA for Section 702 collection, but the ultimate decision to target a non-U.S. person reasonably believed to be located outside the United States rests with NSA.[10] Section 702 is not a bulk collection program; NSA makes an individualized decision with respect to each non-U.S. person target. In addition to this initial targeting decision, the techniques used to acquire the foreign intelligence information pursuant to Section 702 are governed by specific procedures

---

[6] *See, e.g.*, 50 U.S.C. § 1805(c)(2)(A) (requiring all electronic surveillance to be conducted in conformance with "minimization procedures"); 50 U.S.C. § 1825(c)(2)(A) (requiring the same for physical searches); 50 U.S.C. § 1801(h) (defining "minimization procedures" to be, in part, procedures "reasonably designed in light of the purpose and technique of the particular surveillance, to minimize the acquisition ...of nonpublicly available information concerning unconsenting United States persons consistent with the need of the United States to obtain, produce, and disseminate foreign intelligence information."); 50 U.S.C. § 1821(4) (same for physical searches).

[7] Previously released information regarding the sharing of unevaluated FBI-acquired FISA information with CIA may be found at https://icontherecord.tumblr.com/post/112610953998/release-of-documents-concerning-activities-under. The original motion seeking approval for such sharing is *available at* https://www.dni.gov/files/documents/0315/Exhibit%20A%20to%20May%2010%202002%20Motion.pdf.

[8] 50 U.S.C. § 1881a(a), (g).

[9] 50 U.S.C. § 1881a(d). A redacted version of the NSA's targeting procedures is *available at* https://www.dni.gov/files/documents/icotr/51117/2016_NSA_702_Targeting_Procedures_Mar_30_17.pdf (hereinafter "NSA Section 702 Targeting Procedures"). Additional descriptions of the Section 702 targeting process may be found in the NSA Director of Civil Liberties and Privacy Office Report: NSA's Implementation of Foreign Intelligence Surveillance Act Section 702, April 16, 2014, pages 2-6, *available at* http://www.dni.gov/files/documents/0421/702%20Unclassified%20Document.pdf, and the Privacy and Civil Liberties Oversight Board's (PCLOB) "Report on the Surveillance Program Operated Pursuant to Section 702 of the Foreign Intelligence Surveillance Act, July 2, 2014, pages 41-48, *available at* https://www.pclob.gov/library/702-Report.pdf (hereinafter, "PCLOB Report").

[10] *See* PCLOB Report. at 42, 47.

designed to limit the scope of the data collected.[11] In addition, there are statutory limitations on collection activities under Section 702 of FISA that prohibit the Government from (1) intentionally targeting persons known to be located in the United States; (2) intentionally targeting persons reasonably believed to be located outside of the United States, if the purpose is to target an individual reasonably believed to be located within the United States; (3) targeting a U.S. person reasonably believed to be located outside of the United States; (4) intentionally acquiring any communication when the sender and all intended recipients are known at the time of the acquisition of the communication to be located in the United States; and (5) or otherwise acquiring information in a manner inconsistent with the Fourth Amendment to the Constitution.[12]

As described further below, the targeted information that CIA receives from either NSA or FBI pursuant to either Section 702 or Titles I/III of FISA is subject to specific procedures, referred to as "minimization procedures," that are approved by the Attorney General and the FISC and govern access to, retention of, and dissemination of the information. Prior to any dissemination of information concerning U.S. persons, CIA must first determine that the U.S. person information meets the retention requirements. As a result, the limitations and oversight mechanisms governing retention provide important checks prior to any decision to disseminate U.S. person information.

In addition to these specific FISA minimization procedures, CIA's dissemination of information is restricted by the statutory authorities, Executive Order, procedures, and practices that govern and limit all of CIA's foreign intelligence activities. While statutes and Executive Order 12333 provide the general authority for CIA to conduct intelligence activities, CIA does not independently determine its intelligence collection priorities. CIA's intelligence activities are instead conducted in response to intelligence requirements established by the President and CIA's other intelligence consumers. Specifically, the DNI approves the National Intelligence Priorities Framework (NIPF),[13] which establishes national intelligence priorities that reflect the guidance of the President and the National Security Advisor with input from Cabinet-level and other senior government officials. CIA's duly authorized intelligence activities are conducted in response to the NIPF priorities or other intelligence requirements imposed by the President and other intelligence consumers.

---

[11] *See* 50 U.S.C. § 1881a(d)(1)(B) (requiring the adoption of targeting procedures that are reasonably designed to "prevent the intentional acquisition of any communications as to which the sender and all intended recipients are known at the time of the acquisition to be located in the United States."); 50 U.S.C. § 1881a(e)(1) (requiring the adoption of minimization procedures as defined by 50 U.S.C. § 1801(h) or 50 U.S.C. § 1821(4)); *supra* note 6 (providing statutory definitions of minimization procedures); *see also* NSA Section 702 Targeting Procedures, *supra*; NSA's Section 702 Minimization Procedures, § 3, *available at* https://www.dni.gov/files/documents/icotr/51117/2016-NSA-702-Minimization-Procedures_Mar_30_17.pdf.
[12] 50 U.S.C. § 1881a(b).
[13] Information concerning the NIPF is *available at* https://dni.gov/files/documents/ICD/ICD%20204%20National%20Intelligence%20Priorities%20Framework.pdf.

In all activities, including but not limited to FISA, CIA is authorized to disseminate information concerning U.S. persons, only in furtherance of CIA's authorized intelligence activities, or in limited circumstances to provide information indicating a crime or illegal activity to law enforcement agencies that is acquired incidentally while conducting these foreign intelligence activities. CIA may not maintain information for the sole purpose of monitoring the lawful exercise of rights secured by the Constitution or United States law, including First Amendment rights. CIA is also prohibited from engaging in any activities for purposes of affecting or interfering with the domestic political process.[14]

Because these rules and restrictions govern all of CIA's foreign intelligence activities, not just its review of data acquired pursuant to FISA, CIA has a variety of processes, guidelines, and training to ensure the proper handling of all U.S. person information. These practices establish a baseline for the handling, including dissemination, of U.S. person information, which are further supplemented by FISA-specific protections. Relevant aspects of these more general practices pertaining to dissemination are discussed further below.

Finally, but critically, it is important to understand that CIA produces and disseminates to policymakers and partners all-source analysis in order to provide tactical and strategic advantage to the United States. The fact that the information CIA produces may be tactical, strategic, or both is a key feature to understanding how CIA disseminates information, including U.S. person information. In determining what information is to be disseminated to policymakers and partners, including but not limited to U.S. person information, CIA must assess whether the specific U.S. person information is necessary to understand the foreign intelligence information in light of the information that is to be disseminated and the needs and authorities of the recipients of the information.

Consistent with CIA's foreign intelligence mission, this means that U.S. person identifying information (such as a name or title) is often not just deleted or replaced with a generic term, but instead never referenced in the first place in the reporting, which is instead focused on the priorities identified in the NIPF. On the other hand, particularly in instances regarding more "tactical" information that is disseminated to a limited number of individuals or entities directly involved in countering the foreign intelligence threat at issue, CIA personnel may make the determination at the time of dissemination that the U.S. person's information and identity are necessary to understand the foreign intelligence information and will therefore disseminate this identifying information in the first instance, as opposed to deleting the U.S. person information or replacing the U.S. person identity with a generic term. In addition, there are instances in which the U.S. person information is necessary for some recipients to understand the foreign intelligence reporting, but not for others. In this case, CIA deletes or otherwise sanitizes the U.S. person information with a generic term such as "a named U.S. person" for the

---

[14] *See* CIA's Executive Order 12333 Attorney General Procedures, *available at* https://www.cia.gov/about-cia/privacy-and-civil-liberties/CIA-AG-Guidelines-Signed.pdf.

broader audience, while separately providing the specific identity to those individuals or entities for whom that identifying information is necessary.

IV. Procedures Governing CIA's Dissemination of Information Acquired Pursuant to Section 702 and Titles I/III of FISA

As described above, any unevaluated data that CIA receives from either NSA or FBI acquired pursuant to either Section 702 or Titles I/III of FISA must be governed by specific "minimization procedures" adopted by the Attorney General and approved by the FISC, that are reasonably designed to minimize the retention and prohibit the dissemination of non-publicly available information concerning non-consenting U.S. persons, while also remaining consistent with CIA's unique mission requirement of obtaining, producing, and disseminating foreign intelligence information.

CIA has released to the public lightly-redacted versions of the minimization procedures governing both Section 702 collection and Titles I/III collection.[15] In general, the default rule is that information may be disseminated outside of CIA if the information has been determined to be retained under the minimization procedures (as described further below) and "if the identity of the U.S. person and all personally identifiable information regarding the U.S. person are deleted or otherwise sanitized to prevent the search, retrieval or review of the identifying information. A generic term may be substituted which does not identify the U.S. person in the context of the data."[16] In other words, if the information concerning the U.S. person is removed in its entirety or rendered such that the specific U.S. person cannot be identified by the recipient, the information may be disseminated to authorized recipients. Although not a term found in the minimization procedures, as stated above, replacing the U.S. person's identity with a generic term is sometimes colloquially referred to as "masking."

In certain circumstances, however, dissemination of information identifying the U.S. person is permissible. Specifically, the minimization procedures state that if the U.S. person's identity is "necessary to understand foreign intelligence information or assess its importance," the U.S. person's identity may be disseminated to authorized recipients.[17] The minimization

---

[15] CIA's current Section 702 minimization procedures are *available at* https://www.dni.gov/files/documents/icotr/51117/2016_CIA_Section_702_Minimization_Procedures_Se_26_2016. pdf (hereinafter, "CIA Section 702 Minimization Procedures"). Minimization procedures governing CIA's handling of unevaluated Titles I/III data related to terrorism initially acquired by FBI are *available at* https://www.dni.gov/files/documents/0315/Exhibit%20A%20to%20May%2010%202002%20Motion.pdf (hereinafter "CIA Titles I/III Minimization Procedures").

[16] CIA Section 702 Minimization Procedures at § 5; *see also* CIA Titles I/III Minimization Procedures at § 2.

[17] CIA Section 702 Minimization Procedures at § 5; *see also* CIA Titles I/III Minimization Procedures at § 2. The minimization procedures also permit the dissemination of a person's identity that "may become necessary" to

procedures require that in each dissemination CIA evaluates whether the identifying information is necessary to understand the foreign intelligence information.

Prior to dissemination of any information identifying, or even concerning, a U.S. person, the minimization procedures require that CIA make a determination that the information concerning the U.S. person may be retained outside of access-controlled systems accessible only to CIA personnel with specialized FISA training to review unevaluated information. Information regarding a U.S. person may only be retained outside such access-controlled repositories if (a) the information concerning the U.S. person is publicly available; (b) the U.S. person has consented to the retention of the information concerning him or her; (c) the U.S. person's identity is deleted or otherwise sanitized to prevent the search, retrieval or review ("querying") of the identifying information; or (d) the U.S. person's information falls within one of several established categories related to CIA's foreign intelligence mission.[18] These established categories include that the U.S. person information indicates that an individual is an agent of a foreign power (e.g., a member of an international terrorist organization), that the U.S. person may be the target of a foreign power's intelligence activities, or the information concerns a U.S. government official acting in their official capacity.

Certain other rules provide further restrictions with respect to certain disseminations. Strict rules restrict the dissemination of any attorney-client information obtained pursuant to these FISA authorities.[19] Special rules also apply to disseminations of information concerning U.S. persons to a foreign government.[20] CIA is also permitted to disseminate to FBI and other appropriate law enforcement authorities information that reasonably appears to be evidence of a crime.[21] According to CIA OGC, disseminations of FISA information to law enforcement of information that is not foreign intelligence information but is evidence of a crime are rare. None of the disseminated reports reviewed by OPCL contained information that was solely evidence of a crime.

---

understand certain types of foreign intelligence information, such as information concerning international terrorism. In discussions with FISA Program Office personnel, as well as OPCL's review of training materials and actual disseminations, OPCL did not discover any reliance on the "may become necessary" language as a basis for dissemination.

[18] CIA Section 702 Minimization Procedures at § 3; *see also* CIA Titles I/III Minimization Procedures at § 2.

[19] *See* CIA Section 702 Minimization Procedures at § 7(a); *see also* CIA Titles I/III Minimization Procedures at § 4(a).

[20] *See* CIA Section 702 Minimization Procedures at § 7(c); *see also* CIA Titles I/III Minimization Procedures at § 4(e).

[21] *See* CIA Section 702 Minimization Procedures at § 7(d); *see also* CIA Titles I/III Minimization Procedures at § 4(f).

V.   Dissemination in Practice

While CIA minimization procedures set the outer bounds of what is permissible in the dissemination of information concerning the U.S. person, OPCL's review extended to what practices CIA has developed to implement these procedures, as well as the scope and nature of information actually disseminated by CIA. To this end, OPCL met with senior managers from multiple elements who supervise the dissemination of foreign intelligence information, officers in the FISA Program Office who train and oversee CIA's FISA program, and CIA OGC attorneys who review disseminations of U.S. person information. OPCL also reviewed four months of disseminations that had been identified as containing U.S. person information obtained pursuant to Section 702 of FISA.[22]

Consistent with the minimization procedures for Titles I/III and Section 702 of FISA, the protection of U.S. person information begins before a report is drafted for potential dissemination. Unevaluated data is stored in access-controlled repositories and may be viewed only by CIA personnel who have received specific training in the applicable rules for minimizing the long-term retention and dissemination of information concerning U.S. persons.[23]

The "retention decision," a required precursor to the dissemination of any information concerning a U.S. person, is a particularly critical juncture in the minimization process. It is at this stage that information concerning a U.S. person that does not meet one of the specific retention categories outlined in the minimization procedures is removed from the communication before it is made available for dissemination. Such retention decisions are individualized – each communication must be evaluated separately and all information within the communication that is not deleted or replaced with a generic term that does not identify a specific U.S. person must be determined to meet the retention standard. When making these individualized retention decisions, CIA personnel are required to indicate whether any of the information to be retained contains U.S. person identifying information and, if so, the personnel must write a further contemporaneous justification for why the retention of the U.S. person identifying information is permissible under the relevant CIA minimization procedures. These retention justifications are subject to oversight by DOJ and ODNI.

This initial retention decision is necessary but not sufficient to disseminate information concerning U.S. persons. Based on statistics kept by the FISA Program Office, CIA disseminates

---

[22] OPCL did not separately review all similar CIA disseminations in this time period of information acquired by FBI pursuant to Titles I/III of FISA, but some reviewed disseminations of Section 702-acquired information also contained disseminated Titles I/III information.

[23] While CIA's Title I/III minimization procedures do not discuss training, CIA's policy is to require such training, consistent with the requirement in CIA's Section 702 minimization procedures.

a very small percentage of the information concerning U.S. person information that has been determined to meet the retention standard articulated in CIA's minimization procedures.

All such disseminations of U.S. person information acquired pursuant to Section 702 or Titles I/III of FISA are required to be coordinated with several CIA elements prior to dissemination, including a CIA OGC attorney, the FISA Program Office, and a cadre of CIA managers that supervise the dissemination of all information (not just FISA information) concerning U.S. persons. In separate briefings, several CIA senior managers charged with supervising and/or approving the dissemination of information outside of CIA stated that while CIA does disseminate information concerning U.S. person information when it must, these procedural requirements and the greater scrutiny given to any dissemination of U.S. person information act to reinforce the requirement that information identifying a U.S. person be disseminated only when necessary.

OPCL's review of CIA's disseminations identified several commonalities:

- First, OPCL identified no violations of the CIA minimization procedures. In each case, OPCL determined that the information concerning or identifying a U.S. person was necessary to understand the foreign intelligence information contained in the disseminated report. More specifically, the information concerning U.S. persons was necessary to understand specific national security threats identified in both the NIPF and Section 702 certifications approved by the Attorney General and the DNI, not the broader and more theoretical outer limits of FISA's definition of foreign intelligence information. OPCL's findings are consistent with those of past oversight and compliance reviews. Since 2008, DOJ and ODNI have identified no intentional incidents of noncompliance with the use of the FISA Section 702 authorities.[24] While unintentional compliance incidents have occurred, incidents involving CIA's dissemination of U.S. person information are extremely rare.[25]

- Second, CIA's disseminations of FISA-acquired information concerning U.S. persons tended to be both tactical in nature and relatively narrow in distribution. As opposed to general strategic information regarding broad foreign intelligence threats, CIA's disseminations of information concerning U.S. persons were "tactical" insofar as they are

---

[24] *See also* PCLOB Report at 133.
[25] *See, e.g.*, U.S. DEPARTMENT OF JUSTICE, QUARTERLY REPORT TO THE FOREIGN INTELLIGENCE SURVEILLANCE COURT CONCERNING COMPLIANCE MATTERS UNDER SECTION 702 OF THE FOREIGN INTELLIGENCE SURVEILLANCE ACT, March 2015, at 68, *available at* https://www.dni.gov/files/documents/icotr/51117/Bates%20580-671.pdf. (identifying no incidents of noncompliance with the CIA minimization procedures during the reporting period); U.S. DEPARTMENT OF JUSTICE, QUARTERLY REPORT TO THE FOREIGN INTELLIGENCE SURVEILLANCE COURT CONCERNING COMPLIANCE MATTERS UNDER SECTION 702 OF THE FOREIGN INTELLIGENCE SURVEILLANCE ACT, MARCH 2014, at 63, *available at* https://www.dni.gov/files/documents/icotr/51117/Bates%20672-752.pdf (same).

very often in response to requests from another U.S. intelligence agency for counterterrorism information regarding a specific individual, or in relation to a specific national security threat actor or potential or actual victim of a national security threat. As such, reports containing information concerning U.S. persons were disseminated for purposes and in a manner directly related to the specific national security threat at issue. Specifically, the reports were generally disseminated not to the United States Intelligence Community as a whole, but to the participating elements, and sometimes individuals within those elements, who had requested the information or who were working to address the specific national security threat.

- Third, and relatedly, the replacement of a U.S. person identity with a generic term (e.g., "named U.S. person") was rare. Consistent with CIA's foreign intelligence mission, disseminated intelligence products often contain no U.S. person information, as CIA's reporting is focused on foreign intelligence priorities established by the NIPF. As a result, disseminations outside CIA were focused on foreign intelligence information related to non-U.S. persons and the number of reports containing United States person information were few in number.[26] Where dissemination of information concerning U.S. person information did occur, however, U.S. persons were generally specifically identified because the identities were determined to be necessary to understand the foreign intelligence information by the relatively narrow list of entities or individuals who received CIA's report.

- Fourth, CIA also produces finished intelligence products to policymakers and broader audiences within the Intelligence Community of a more strategic nature. The broader scope and audience of these documents, combined with CIA's *foreign* intelligence mission, however, often results in the deletion, not the replacement with a generic term, of information concerning U.S. persons. When appropriate, generic terms such as "named U.S. person" or "named U.S. company" are utilized. CIA's Directorate of Analysis advises that it rarely receives requests for the specific identities behind such generic terms, and in the rare instances when this does occur, the requests are referred to the CIA entity that initially reviewed the acquired communications. In order to subsequently identify, i.e., "unmask," the U.S. persons to anyone outside CIA, CIA personnel would need to reapply both the retention and dissemination procedures discussed above and issue a new report with a narrower audience containing the identifying information.

---

[26] In a substantial proportion of these disseminations, the U.S. person identified was a U.S. corporation or organization, not an individual. FISA's definition of "United States person," extends not only to United States citizens and lawful permanent residents, but also to corporations incorporated in the United States and unincorporated associations where a substantial number of members are United States citizens or lawful permanent residents. 50 U.S.C. § 1801(i).

OPCL identified no such "unmaskings" in the four months of reports containing FISA-acquired information it reviewed.

In summary, CIA's privacy and civil liberties protections with regard to disseminating U.S. person information are not best described with reference to the "masking" or "unmasking" of individuals. While the use of generic terms is sometimes utilized, the more critical controls for protecting U.S. person information occur in the initial targeting and collection, the retention decisions regarding which information may be kept that are made as a prerequisite to any dissemination, the exclusion of irrelevant information concerning U.S. persons in disseminations, and the determination of the appropriate list of recipients for whom reporting identifying specific U.S. persons is determined to be necessary to understand the foreign intelligence information.

VI. Training

CIA takes a multi-pronged approach in its training to ensure compliance with the procedures and practices for disseminating information concerning U.S. persons only when appropriate. In the first instance, CIA's handling of U.S. person information must comply with CIA's Executive Order 12333 Attorney General Procedures. All new CIA officers receive training on the Attorney General Procedures. In addition, CIA personnel who manage the reporting of intelligence information outside of CIA receive additional, specialized training that focuses on the restrictions on disseminating information concerning U.S. persons.

Because FISA has additional, more specific, rules that may supersede some of the requirements of the Attorney General Procedures, all CIA personnel who have access to unevaluated information acquired under FISA are required to receive additional, in-person training provided by CIA OGC and the FISA Program Office. This training covers, but is not limited to, the restrictions governing the retention and dissemination of U.S. person information. OPCL assesses that CIA's FISA training program provides practical guidance to trainees regarding the application of the CIA minimization procedures and related CIA policies. For example, trainees are provided specific examples of sufficient and insufficient justifications for retaining information concerning a U.S. person, the precursor decision for any dissemination of a U.S. person identity. The role of subsequent oversight is also emphasized. Trainees are repeatedly reminded that their retention and dissemination decisions are subject to additional external review by DOJ and ODNI.

Supervisors who manage CIA's reporting of foreign intelligence information emphasized that these formal training requirements are supplemented by on-the-job training. Junior officers are provided guidance from more experienced officers in honing their skills to make the determination of what is, in fact, necessary to understand the foreign intelligence information. In addition, CIA OGC attorneys are integrated with mission elements to provide further guidance to

14

CIA personnel and the FISA Program Office provides additional resources regarding the dissemination of U.S. person information.

VII. Compliance and Oversight

In the first instance, compliance with the regulations and procedures governing the dissemination of U.S. person information is monitored by CIA managers specifically trained in the dissemination of information outside of CIA. In the case of information acquired pursuant to Titles I/III and Section 702 of FISA, all disseminations concerning U.S. persons also must be coordinated with CIA OGC attorneys and the FISA Program Office. Both CIA OGC attorneys and FISA Program Office staff advised that they will request further information on a report prior to concurring in the dissemination if it appears that any of the FISA-acquired information concerning an identified U.S. person is not necessary to understand the foreign intelligence information.

In addition, DOJ and ODNI conduct bimonthly reviews of CIA's compliance with the Section 702 minimization procedures. These Section 702 oversight reviews include an evaluation of retention decisions (including the contemporaneous written justifications of such retention decisions) and a review of all CIA reports that disseminate information concerning an identified U.S. person. DOJ has reviewed disseminations of United States person information acquired pursuant to the Title I/III in the past and is discussing with CIA the conduct of future reviews.

On a more programmatic basis, CIA's handling of U.S. person information in FISA and other contexts is also subject to review by OPCL, as occurred during the course of this review, and by CIA's Office of the Inspector General. The Privacy and Civil Liberties Oversight Board also conducted a comprehensive review of the FISA Section 702 program.[27]

Oversight is also conducted by Congress and the judiciary. The FISC must approve Section 702 certifications and all FISA Title I/III applications, to include the minimization procedures that govern all collection obtained from those certifications/applications. Incidents of potential noncompliance with the CIA's minimization procedures are reported to DOJ, which in turn reports confirmed incidents of non-compliance to the FISC and to Congress. Compliance incidents involving CIA's dissemination of U.S. person information are exceedingly rare, but when a compliance incident of any type is discovered, this incident report describes the scope, nature, and the cause of the incident.

---

[27] (U) *See* PCLOB Report, *supra* note 9.

15

VIII. Conclusion

OPCL's review of CIA's dissemination of information concerning U.S. persons initially acquired by NSA and FBI pursuant to Section 702 and Titles I/III of FISA revealed no incidents of noncompliance with the applicable procedures governing such disseminations. Consistent with CIA's foreign intelligence mission, the disseminated reports were all in response to specific, identifiable foreign intelligence priorities and identifying information concerning U.S. persons was only released to authorized persons outside of CIA when that identifying information was necessary to understand the foreign intelligence information. CIA has specific procedures, practices, training, and oversight to ensure the appropriate dissemination of U.S. person information.

Updated Guide to Posted Documents Regarding Use of National Security Authorities – as of December 4, 2017

Set forth below are links to certain officially released documents related to the use by the Intelligence Community (IC) of national security authorities. These documents have been published to meet legal requirements, as well as to carry out the *Principles of Intelligence Transparency for the IC*. Listed below are links to selected documents; there are many more officially released documents available for public review.

* New or updated entries are denoted with an asterisk.

IC on the Record. IC on the Record (ICOTR) is an online platform maintained by the Office of the Director of National Intelligence (ODNI) to provide officially released information about the IC, focusing primarily on foreign intelligence surveillance activities. Hundreds of documents and thousands of pages have been posted on this platform.

- **ICOTR Transparency Tracker:** The ODNI's Office of Civil Liberties, Privacy and Transparency maintains the ICOTR Transparency Tracker. This spreadsheet indexes the materials posted on IC on the Record, as well as relevant materials posted on other government sites.

***Intelligence.gov.** Intelligence.gov (or Intel.gov) is an all-new digital front door for the U.S. Intelligence Community, with a focus on increasing transparency about the IC's authorities and activities. It works alongside ICOTR and other IC resources—including the websites of IC agencies—to provide clear and accurate information about the IC.

  - **Intel Vault.** Intel.gov includes the Intel Vault, which enables the public to explore repositories of officially released information about the IC. It includes the capability to conduct full text searches on a database of the Section 702 documents posted on ICOTR.

General Overviews of Section 702 of the Foreign Intelligence Surveillance Act (FISA). The FISA Amendments Act – which includes Section 702- will expire at the end of 2017 unless it is reauthorized by Congress. The government has provided general overviews of this critical national security authority:

- **FISA Amendments Act: Q&A.** The IC prepared a detailed Q&A document describing Section 702 and other provisions of the FISA Amendments Act. This document includes a discussion of the intelligence value of Section 702, with examples.

- **Joint Unclassified Statement on Section 702.** IC FISA experts testified about Section 702 before the House Judiciary Committee in March, 2017. The statement for the record provides a detailed overview of Section 702, and is posted here.

- **IC Legal Reference Book.** The text of FISA and other legal authorities relevant to the IC can be found in the IC Legal Reference Book, compiled by ODNI's Office of the General Counsel.

- ***NSA's Q&A on Section 702.** NSA prepared a guide to Section 702 in question-and-answer format: Understanding the Impact of Section 702 on the Typical American.

- ***Guide to Section 702 Value Examples.** ODNI prepared a guide to officially released information on the value of information collected under Section 702.

Reports on Use of National Security Authorities. The government prepares a variety of reports detailing its use of national security authorities. These reports contain a wealth of information about how the government implements FISA and other key authorities.

- **Annual Statistical Transparency Report Regarding Us of National Security Authorities.** For the past four years, the ODNI has published on ICOTR annual reports that provide important statistics on how national security authorities are used. The fourth such report, for calendar year 2016, is posted here. This report includes statistics required by the USA FREEDOM Act, as well as other statistics published pursuant to the *Principles of Intelligence Transparency*.

- **Reports posted on the Privacy and Civil Liberties Oversight Board's website** (www.pclob.gov). The Privacy and Civil Liberties Oversight Board (PCLOB) is an independent, bipartisan agency within the executive branch. The PCLOB provides advice and oversight regarding efforts to protect the Nation from terrorism. The PCLOB has published major reports on the executive branch's use of national security authorities.
    - PCLOB Report on the Surveillance Program Operated Pursuant to Section 702 of FISA (July 2, 2014).
    - PCLOB Report on the Telephone Records Program Conducted under Section 215 of the USA PATRIOT Act and on the Operations of the Foreign Intelligence Surveillance Court (January 23, 2014).
    - PCLOB Update on the government's implementation of the PCLOB Recommendations on Section 215 and Section 702 (February 5, 2016).

- **Reports posted on NSA's Civil Liberties and Privacy Office (NSA CLPO) website** (www.nsa.gov/about/civil-liberties). NSA CLPO has, in the interest of transparency, prepared and published three reports describing how NSA implements key authorities, and assessing the corresponding civil liberties and privacy implications.
    - NSA CLPO Report on NSA's implementation of Section 702.
    - NSA CLPO Transparency Report on NSA's implementation of the new business records provisions of the USA FREEDOM Act.
    - NSA CLPO Report on civil liberties and privacy protections for targeted signals intelligence (SIGINT) activities under Executive Order 12333.

- ***Reports on Protecting U.S. Person Identities in FISA Disseminations.** ODNI posted reports on ICOTR that review how intelligence agencies protect the identities of U.S. persons when disseminating information collected under FISA. These reports were prepared, at the direction of the DNI, by the civil liberties and privacy officers for the ODNI, NSA, FBI, and CIA.
  - ODNI Report on Protecting U.S. Person Identities in Disseminations under FISA
  - Annex 1 - The National Security Agency's (NSA) Report
  - Annex 2 - The Federal Bureau of Investigation's (FBI) Report
  - Annex 3 - The Central Intelligence Agency's (CIA) Report
  - Annex 4 - The National Counterterrorism Center's (NCTC) Report

Targeting and Minimization under Section 702 of FISA. The government has released court-approved targeting and minimization procedures under Section 702.

- **Targeting Procedures.** Section 702 allows for the targeting of (i) non-United States persons (ii) reasonably believed to be located abroad (iii) to acquire foreign intelligence information. Targeting is effectuated by tasking communications facilities (such as telephone numbers and electronic communications accounts) to U.S. electronic communications service providers. For the first time, the government released redacted versions of targeting procedures.
  - 2016 NSA's Section 702 Targeting Procedures dated March 30, 2017
  - 2016 FBI's Section 702 Targeting Procedures dated September 26, 2016

- **Minimization Procedures.** Section 702 also requires minimization procedures to minimize and protect any non-publicly available information concerning unconsenting United States persons that may be incidentally collected when appropriately targeting non-United States persons abroad for foreign intelligence information. The government has released several sets of minimization procedures for the past few years. The most recently released minimization procedures are set forth below.
  - 2016 NSA's Section 702 Minimization Procedures dated March 30, 2017
  - 2016 FBI's Section 702 Minimization Procedures dated September 26, 2016
  - 2016 CIA's Section 702 Minimization Procedures dated September 26, 2016
  - 2016 NCTC's Section 702 Minimization Procedures dated September 26, 2016

Compliance, Oversight, and Other Documents under Section 702. The government has released other relevant documents, including those relating to the extensive compliance and oversight measures undertaken under Section 702.

- **Summary of Oversight Activities Conducted by DOJ and ODNI.** The National Security Division of the Department of Justice and the ODNI jointly conduct oversight of how the IC implements Section 702. These activities were officially described a filing with the FISC, which is posted here.

- **2015 Summary of Notable Section 702 Requirements.** This summary serves as a reference guide to certain notable requirements relating to the IC's implementation of Section 702. This summary is posted here.

- **Semiannual Assessments of Compliance with Procedures and Guidelines Issued Pursuant to Section 702 of FISA. Semiannual Compliance Assessments under Section 702 of FISA.** These compliance assessments are jointly submitted by the Attorney General and the DNI. As of January 2017, fifteen joint assessments have been submitted. The 13th-15th Joint Assessments are posted here, together with a corresponding Fact Sheet explaining joint assessments.

- **NSA Guidance and Training Documents.** NSA has released certain documents that provide guidance and/or training for NSA personnel in implementing Section 702.
  - NSA's 702 Targeting Review Guidance
  - NSA's 702 Practical Applications Training
  - NSA's 702 Training for NSA Adjudicators
  - NSA's 702 Adjudication Checklist
  - NSA's Training on FISA Amendments Act Section 702

- **DOJ Memorandum on Restriction Regarding the Use of FISA Section 702 Information in Criminal Proceedings Against United States Persons.** This memorandum from the National Security Division of the Department of Justice is posted here.

Recently Posted Opinions of the Foreign Intelligence Surveillance Court (FISC) and the Foreign Intelligence Surveillance Court of Review (FISCR). The FISC and FISCR carry out their judicial duties under FISA in a classified setting, so that they can receive and act on classified information relating to the government's implementation of FISA authorities. Recently, a substantial number of filings, rulings, and other documents related to the FISC and FISCR have been made public, in redacted form.

- **FISC Website.** FISC rulings, filings and other documents can also be found on the FISC's website: http://www.fisc.uscourts.gov/.

- **Recent Releases on ICOTR.**
  - The FISC's April 26, 2017 Memorandum Opinion and Order, addressing, among other things, the upstream compliance incident that is described by NSA here.
  - Over a dozen FISC opinions and related documents, recently released as part of FOIA litigation.
  - Release of FISC Question of Law and FISCR Opinion, regarding collection of post-cut through digits using a pen register and trap and trace device.
  - Release of three FISC opinions:[1]

---

[1] This reference has been broken out so that there are now separate links to each opinion.

- - June 18, 2015 Memorandum Opinion regarding appointment of amicus for a particular case.
  - November 6, 2015 Memorandum Opinion and Order regarding the 2015 Section 702 Certifications, including review of the legality of U.S. person queries. Other documents relating to the above include:[2]
    - *FISC Order appointing amicus
    - *Amicus brief
    - *Government's brief in response to briefing order
    - *Transcript of oral argument
    - *Note that Annual Statistical Transparency Report, at page 10, includes the results of the reporting ordered in the FISC's November 6, 2015 opinion, at pages 44 and 78.
  - December 31, 2015 Memorandum Opinion, approving the Government's first application for orders requiring the production of call detail records under the USA FREEDOM Act.
- FISC documentation relating to 2011 certifications originally posted in 2013, with additional documents released in 2017.
- Links to the FISC documentation relating to 2016 certifications, and other FISA documents, are included in this comprehensive posting.

Executive Order 12333. The IC has also released important documents related to Executive Order 12333, which establishes the Executive Branch framework for the country's national intelligence efforts, and includes safeguards for protecting privacy and civil liberties in the conduct of intelligence activities. It was originally issued by President Ronald Reagan in 1981, was most recently revised and re-issued by President George W. Bush in 2008.

- **General Documents.** Executive Order 12333, as amended, is posted here. An information paper describing the 2008 revision is posted here.

- **Attorney-General Approved Procedures.** Section 2.3 of Executive Order 12333 provides that IC elements may collect, retain, and disseminate information concerning United States persons pursuant to procedures established by the head of the IC element and approved by the Attorney General, in consultation with the DNI.
  - **DoD.** The Department of Defense updated its Attorney General-approved procedures last year: Department of Defense Manual 5240.01, Procedures Governing the Conduct of DoD Intelligence Activities.[3]
  - These procedures cover the IC elements that are part of DoD: DIA, NGA, NRO, NSA, and the intelligence elements of the Army, Navy, Air Force, and Marines.

---

[2] These links are newly included to facilitate identification of these documents, which were released and posted on ICOTR in April 2017.

[3] Link has been updated.

- **NSA.** In addition, NSA also follows United States Signals Directive (USSID) SP0018, Legal Compliance and U.S. Persons Minimization Procedures (January 25, 2011), commonly referred to as USSID 18.
- **CIA.** The CIA updated its Attorney General approved procedures earlier this year: CIA's Executive Order 12333, Attorney General Procedures, with corresponding Detailed Description.
- **FBI.** The FBI operates under the Attorney General's Guidelines for Domestic FBI Operations. A detailed Domestic Investigations and Operations Guide provides specific guidance for implementing the guidelines.
- **Table.** A table with links to IC elements' procedures is posted here.

- **Raw Signals Intelligence Availability Procedures.** Section 2.3 of Executive Order 12333 also provides that raw or unminimized signals intelligence (SIGINT) information may only be disseminated or made available to IC elements in accordance with procedures established by the DNI in coordination with the Secretary of Defense and approved by the Attorney General. The Raw SIGINT Availability Procedures were finalized and released in January of this year, and are posted here, with corresponding Fact Sheet. The procedures require strict safeguards comparable to those of NSA for handling such information.

Presidential Policy Directive 28, Signals Intelligence Activities (PPD-28). PPD-28 was issued in January 2014 and remains in effect. It sets forth general privacy protection principles for SIGINT activities, limits the use of SIGINT collected in bulk, provides for the involvement of senior policy makers in key SIGINT decisions, and imposes specific safeguards to protect the privacy of all individuals, regardless of nationality.

- **PPD-28.** PPD-28 is posted here.

- **IC Element Policies Implementing PPD-28.** Section 4 of PPD-28 calls on each IC element to update existing or issue new policies and procedures to implement principles for safeguarding all personal information collected through SIGINT, consistent with technical capabilities and operational needs. A table with links to each IC element's policies under PPD-28 is posted here. In addition, links to two IC Standards relating to PPD-28 are posted here.

- **Annual Signals Intelligence Reform Progress Report.** For the past three years, the ODNI has published an annual report outlining progress under PPD-28 and related SIGINT reform efforts. The report for calendar year 2016 is posted here.

Gates Procedures. The Gates Procedures provide that, unless a specific exception applies, prior approval must be obtained from the Office of the Director of National Intelligence if information identifying Members or their staff by name or by individually identifying titles or characteristics (congressional identity information) is included in intelligence reports being

6

disseminated to Executive Branch entities outside of the requesting IC element. A statement providing the background for these procedures is posted here. The procedures are contained in an annex to IC Directive 112, Congressional Notification, and are posted here.